for
Remember His Name

Judith Finneren has created a beautiful book, a deeply engaging, heartfelt journey as she navigates the unknown waters of profound loss. *Remember His Name* is touching, inspirational and a true gift for the loving and healing heart.
Kristine Carlson, Don't Sweat the Small Stuff books

Judith Finneren's book, *Remember His Name,* is about healing, hope and moving on after a devastating loss. Judith shares her personal experiences and leaves the reader feeling inspired and hopeful.
Christina Rasmussen, author of *Second firsts: Live, Laugh and Love Again*

I highly recommend *Remember His Name* to anyone coping with the tragedy, pain, and grief that follows losing a loved one. Judith's journey after the untimely death of her husband offers hope and inspiration to those going through similar circumstances when healing and hope seems unattainable. For those facing the challenge, her story will serve to shift your perspective.
Sarah McLean, author of *The Power of Attention: Awaken to Love and its Unlimited Potential with Meditation*

Remember His Name

Conquering Sorrow, Accepting Joy

Judith Finneren

Remember His Name
Copyright © 2017 Judith Finneren
All rights reserved.

Book cover design by Judith Finneren and Denise Cassino
Book cover photo by Zach Urness
Back cover Author photo by Gary Ishmael
Book cover photo owner Grants Pass Daily Courier
Editing by Eye Comb Editors (www.eyecombeditors.com)
and Sojourn Publishing, LLC

Judith Finneren books are available for order through
Amazon.com.
Visit my website: judithfinneren.com
Follow me on twitter: @judithfinneren
Connect with me on Facebook: Judith M. Finneren

Printed in the United States of America
First Printing: July 2017
Published by: Dancing Bear Publishing

Paperback ISBN: 978-1-62747-106-0
Kindle ISBN: 978-1-62747-108-4

Dedication

Dedicated to my love, my life, my world,
always and forever,
Ralph Dennis Finneren.
Thank you for teaching me what
love is.

And
to our children,
Rory and Holli Finneren,
who continue teaching me what love is.

Ralph Finneren

Rory and Holli Finneren

Contents

Acknowledgments

Gratitude and love to the many friends, family, strangers, and spirits who helped create this book. I am beyond grateful to so many who have supported me and stood by me.

First and foremost, I owe a huge debt of gratitude to my friend and current love of my life, Gary Ishmael, who literally sat by me with absolute solid love and support through each and every step of turning this book into a reality.

My two children, Rory and Holli Finneren, have been my greatest strength and encouragement. Their courage in the face of such tragedy and grief, along with their passion to live life to the fullest, blesses and holds me up, gifting me with pure joy and the courage to take the next step.

The Finneren and Miller families touched my heart from the moment I received the tragic news. Thank you for loving me and being there for me.

I appreciate my loving, cuddly dog, Charlie Jo, who is always ready to hear what I write and, with a wagging tail and barks, reminds me to take breaks for walks.

I want to thank the Tom Bird family: Tom Bird, Sabrina Fritts, Mary Stevenson, and John Hodgkinson, for without their continued support from the bare beginnings through completion, my dream of publishing a book would not have been realized.

I would like to thank those whose help, support and guidance brought this book to fruition, including Rama, Denise

Cassino, David Thalberg, and all the authors and authors-to-be I met on this journey.

Tori Yabo of Eye Comb Editors delivered her uncanny skills that resonated so completely with my mission and message. Your patience, advice, and feedback have been remarkable.

There are so many people to thank for the role they have played in my healing: my two best friends since twelve years of age, Ann Neesley Pattison and Diane Collins; longtime friend Cathy Chambers for believing in me and always asking how the book was coming along; and the many friends and family members who are excited to read *Remember His Name*.

Three mornings a week Phil and Gwen kept my body moving through regular exercise. I am so thankful for that, for I had somewhere to go, people to be with and the gift of taking good care of myself.

Enocha Ranjita Ryan, Martha Edwards, Janet Akers, Christina Rasmussen, Sarah McLean, Barb David, Melanie Wolf, Judith Trenkamp, Kathy McMinn, Michael Mirdad, Pastor Marge Munger, Deputy Harry Joseph, and Marcia Keller are more angels here on earth who played key roles in my healing from loss to feeling whole again.

Special thanks to the League of Michigan Bicyclists, Executive Director John Lindenmayer and Tour Director Scott Elliott, lmb.org. Also, Tim Potter, Sustainable Transportation Manager at MSU bikes, and Mark Hager, Tribute Ride Coordinator at Ride of Silence. Your kindness and support has meant the world to me.

To those whose name I have not mentioned, and there are many, I thank you for helping and supporting me on this journey. You may not realize how much your smiles, your willingness to come to my house, and your courage to sit with me kept me going. My heart is full of gratitude.

Finally, to my readers, those who have lost a loved one and those supporting those who have lost a loved one: thank you for choosing this book, for being brave, for being courageous, for going that extra mile to help yourself and others in the time of greatest human need.

Introduction

I share the story of my husband's passing to help others understand grief, and to help their healing and mine. If you have lost a spouse, you are not alone. This book offers hope, practical tips, courage, and blessings to keep moving forward. Please use the blank page at the end of each chapter to write out your thoughts and feelings. It will be identified with this symbol.

Chapter One
Spiritually Speaking

*A*fter experiencing the death of my beloved husband of thirty-seven years, I began asking myself these questions: *Will I ever feel Ralph's presence? Will his spirit leave clues, such as pennies or feathers, as I have heard happened to so many others?* I did feel Ralph's spirit connect with mine in the weeks immediately following his death. The first few weeks felt chaotic, confusing, and numb. I felt that Ralph and I were feeling the same thing. We both had to accept what happened to feel some peace again and move forward, he in the spiritual realm, and I here on earth.

Some interesting things happened in our home involving electricity. First, at the funeral home during his service, the lights blinked. I felt chills throughout my body, and I knew in my heart it was my Ralph. I felt so comforted knowing his spirit was right there with me.

A friend was gracious enough to stay with me in the six weeks following the funeral. I am so grateful and truly believe that played a role in my being able to maintain breath, a sense of hope, and a future life. One night, my friend and I were chatting in the family room of my tri-level home. We began hearing an unusual sound, that of a radio, we thought. It lasted only a moment, so we continued our chat, forgetting about it until the following evening, where again we were chatting. This time, the sound occurred again, louder and for a longer

1

time. We still let it pass as unusual, not really concerned. By the third night, the sound got so loud and lasted so long that we had to investigate. Flashlights in hand, dog at our side, we followed the sound. It was coming from the garage. We opened the door and, lo and behold, a radio that had belonged to Ralph was playing NPR as it sat on his workbench. We were amazed and startled, realizing that this was Ralph letting us know he was present. Again I felt chills, then a warmth and comfort from my Ralph. Indeed, he was connecting with me. I did not even know he had a radio in the garage, for I never heard him playing it, and he really did not spend much time there. We unplugged the radio and solemnly walked back into the house. We chatted at length in pure amazement at the unexpected visit from Ralph's spirit.

As I write this I am in awe and realize how much, since his death, that he has played a role in helping all of us heal. As he has moved forward in the spiritual realm, we have also moved forward in the earthly realm. It was scary and freaky at first, accepting the truth of all this. I have read several accounts similar to this from many widows and widowers. I also know of many books with amazing accounts of those who have left us, letting us know their spirit is always with us.

Another incident that occurred during the six weeks my friend was with me involves water and electricity. In front of my home, Ralph and I had a fountain, an angel with a book open on her lap with water trickling down. It made a calming sound. Ralph and I loved sitting out in front swinging in our new wooden swing with the sound of the water in the background. I had not had this fountain plugged in since Ralph's death; I could not bear it. My friend and I had gone out for dinner; on our return, I almost fainted. My friend noticed my look of surprise and asked, "What? What?"

"The fountain is lit up, the water is flowing," I said. "What is going on? How is this happening?" I immediately felt Ralph's presence again, just as with the radio playing in the garage. Somehow the fountain was plugged in.

Later on, thinking about this while settling in for the night, I was in awe! Ralph knew how much I loved that fountain. He was reassuring me. My whole body shuddered at the sight. I felt warmth, comfort, and gratitude to Ralph's spirit for letting me know he was here. I felt a little giddy, and as a smile came across my face, I realized I felt happy.

Before Ralph passed, before this life-changing tragedy, I believe Spirit—that is, God—was communicating with us. I say this now, after all that has happened. At the time Spirit was communicating, though, I had no idea. Several things occurred, almost as if the angel of death was hovering near us often in the months before the actual death.

The first time this happened was in our home town, about thirty miles north of Detroit. My cell phone was suddenly missing. Mine was dark purple; Ralph's was black, and they were hard to tell apart. We figured out Ralph had gone on a bicycle ride with my phone in the back of his riding-jersey pocket, and it had fallen out. A young man from Detroit had found it while visiting our hometown for the weekend, so Ralph ended up driving to a high-crime area in Detroit alone to pick up the phone. I was so scared the whole time he was gone and cannot believe I allowed him to go alone. It could have been a set-up. That first incident—where I felt death was knocking on the door—left me feeling shaken.

The next three occurred up North in East Tawas, Michigan, where we have a cute little cabin across from the sparkling blue waters of Lake Huron. I had made arrangements earlier in the year for us to be lighthouse keepers. We had the third week in May, Friday to Friday. The lighthouse had eighty-five stairs up to the Fresnel lens. One benefit of being a lighthouse keeper was being able to stay in a little apartment with a full bath, kitchen, and bedroom right in the lighthouse. It was really cool! The lower level consisted of a museum with historical facts and artifacts. People would come to this beautiful Michigan state park to tour the lighthouse, enjoy the woods and walk along the vast shoreline. Our job was to take people to the top and answer questions.

One night after we had gone to bed, Ralph was sleeping soundly, and I heard someone lightly knocking on the door, and voices. I woke up my husband and said, "There is someone outside." He didn't really wake up or seem concerned, and the noise outside quieted, so I let it go and went to sleep. The next night, Ralph awakened me as I had woken him the night before. Well, this time the noise was louder, a powerful banging noise on the door below, and by now it was around midnight. Ralph ran down the stairs and yelled at the people to leave and stop trying to get into the lighthouse. He yelled upstairs to me, "Call 911!" I was terrified, and in my panic I mistakenly dialed 411, which is for information. For the life of me, I could not figure out why the lady did not seem to care as I explained what was happening. Eventually she understood the situation and got the park rangers to come to our aid. No sheriff or police ever showed up. Ralph and I were both pretty upset, and we decided to head back to our cabin less than a mile away, where our dog was watching over the place. The next day, we had calmed down and returned to our lighthouse keeping duties. Ralph had been so upset, saying there could have been a homicide last night had he opened the door, and that he had decided not to open the door only because of me. (Yeah, me!) Was this the angel of death visiting again? Later, warm, sunny June beckoned us to kayak, one of our favorite things to do. We ventured out in Lake Huron, one of the most crystal clear blue-green of the five great lakes. Waves are known to go from small to large in a moment. It was a calm day, so we kayaked from the state park to uptown. We beached the kayaks, secured them, grabbed lunch, and enjoyed the mild breeze and small-town atmosphere. About two hours later, we decided it was time to head back to the state park. The lake was a little rougher now than when we had arrived. About a third of the way back, the waves grew, and I was getting frightened for both of us. I saw a man waving and a big Coast Guard boat approaching. They told us some people in the area were getting their kayaks stolen and asked us to put some stickers on ours so as to identify them. So we did, and off we went. I told Ralph, "I am going to pull up on shore; I don't like these waves." So Ralph kayaked back to the state park alone. I was praying the whole time, in fear for his life, since by now the waves were pretty rough. He made it, loaded up his kayak into the car and came to pick me up.

We watched the Fourth of July parade that year in this little town up north on Tawas Bay. As we were waiting for it to begin, we noticed this little caterpillar inching its way across the busy four-lane road where the parade was about to begin. We were scared for him and cheered him on to make it across. We were going to run into the road and save him, but a horse's hoof found his little fragile body. We were sad and felt bad that we did not jump up and save him. This stands out in my mind, as I don't remember ever having an experience like this where the both of us were feeling so connected to a tiny life force.

I believe it was this same trip up north where I was driving our little Smart car and a lady rear-ended us. No one was hurt, just shaken up.

These are all incidents that in hindsight lead me to think, *What the heck was going on? Are these pieces all linked or random happenings? Visits from death?* At the time, they were just random things that happen in life. Now, I don't know.

What was happening to us in May, June, and July of 2011?

A week before the day of Ralph's death, on the previous Wednesday, I broke into unstoppable tears, sobs, like my heart was broken. I didn't know why. Then again on Sunday, I began sobbing and crying uncontrollably in our backyard swimming pool that we normally enjoyed so much. That day, it was a refreshing dip after our intense bike ride. I remember I was feeling very alone, as if I had no one in my life who really cared. I even said, "If I died today, no one would come to my funeral." Ralph comforted me, gently, kindly. We sat on the edge of the pool, our legs dangling into the water. I sobbed hard. Ralph offered to run into the house and grab some tissues. He brought them and sat by me, comforting me. It was as if he knew something was about to happen. I now believe he was comforting me for what was to happen the next Wednesday. I don't believe we knew on this earthly plane, but spiritually something was happening.

The Monday that followed, July 25, 2011, was also an interesting evening. Earlier that year, I had discovered a love for filmmaking, working as an extra in a couple of local films. This particular evening, a student filmmaker sent out a message requesting extras for his film. He needed people to be funeral mourners at a local church. I was excited and told Ralph all about it. It was his chance to be an extra with me, since it was happening in the evening and he did not have to work. I don't think he was too keen on being a funeral mourner, but he knew how excited I was, and he went with me. We went, all dressed for a funeral, and sat in the pews at this church. Ralph was wearing my favorite color shirt -- purple. We listened to people talk at the service and we walked in the chapel so the camera people could get the best shots. As we exited the chapel into the lobby, we each were directed to pretend to pick up a rock from a basket full of rocks. I noticed Ralph held a rock in his hand that bore the title of the film, *When You Remember Me, I Hope You Smile*. He was the only one who held a rock in his hand, for he had missed the direction to only pretend to pick one up. The irony of this, as I look back on our last week together, is unbelievable. Was this the final sign? We left that church in a great mood. It was a fun experience we both enjoyed. We had driven our little red Smart car that we'd named "The Cozy Coupe." It was our fun car. We stopped at McDonald's on the way home and each got a Happy Meal. We had so much fun together, and oh, how I miss that!

The next evening as I was driving home from work, I looked to my left, and jogging on the path toward our home was my Ralph. I got butterflies in my tummy and just smiled. Ever since I met him in the fall of 1973, I got butterflies. Our love was so deep, so strong, so meant-to-be. I arrived in our driveway, and shortly thereafter in came Ralph. We had tilapia for dinner, and oh, was it outstandingly delicious! He was the best cook!

Then that fated Wednesday arrived, and a numb feeling cruised through my body. The terror, the horror, the disbelief that it's all real still affects me, body and mind.

Chapter Two
Reminiscing

*W*here do I begin to tell the story of how great a love can be—a true love story that feels older than the sea? A warm summer sun was setting in July, 2011. Now that we had been empty-nesters for over six years with retirement approaching, it was time to talk about our future bliss. We were enjoying time on the wooden swing we purchased a couple months prior. I love that swing. I had wanted one for years and we finally bought one for the front lawn of the home where we'd raised our children. So many special memories bubbled up as my husband and I looked at the basketball net and remembered family games of "Horse" and "Around the World." Laughs, giggles, and screams echoed in our memories.

We reminisced about our first meeting so many years ago. We met in August, 1973, right before my senior year of high school. I was a seventeen-year-old girl, he a man of twenty. We fell in love the first night we met. We dated for a little over a year before we married young. Our first date was sailing on his Hobie 16 catamaran. Oh, my gosh, was that ever fun, and oh my gosh, did I ever get sunburned! The cool breeze kept me from feeling the sun's heat. His sailboat was close to the same color as his cute little Fiat. He loved the color green. Our second date was going to a movie in Birmingham, Michigan, where he lived. We saw *Harold and Maude*. It has Cat Stevens music in it, and we so enjoyed it. Afterward we went to a restaurant named Mon Jin Lau. We ate Chinese, and it was my first time ever. I loved it. We also enjoyed a two-person drink that came with two long straws. As we talked and enjoyed our food, sipping the drink every once in a while, I began to smell something burning. Oh, my gosh, the end of my straw caught on fire by the nearby candle! We laughed and extinguished the fire on the table, but a new one ignited within us. We were falling in love, and we both knew it. Within the first couple of weeks of knowing one another, a postcard arrived for me: "The moment you walked inside my door, I knew I need not look no more, I have seen many other girls before, but darling, heaven must have programmed you." Warm tears of memories, love, and joy trickle down my cool cheek as I remember and am taken back to 1973.

I remember at the end of dates, we would pull up to my house and he would sing "Happy Trails" to me, a song by Roy Rogers and Dale Evans. We would hug and kiss good night, until the next time. I will never ever forget those nights and will cherish them forever. His long, wavy brown hair made my insides giggle, I loved it so. Cute, cute, cute is what he was. He drove a little kiwi-green Fiat. I loved that car too! I would sit on my porch and wait for him to come over. I would hear him turning the corner a block away. The Fiat two-seater had such a unique sound. I felt butterflies every time I saw him and still do, even when I am just thinking about him and feeling the love we shared.

We talked about working and going to college, then the life-changing marvelous events of bringing children into the world. March of 1982 brought us a wonderful son, and January of 1987, an adorable daughter. Now we missed them so, for our lives had been full of family activities for many years: soccer, karate, gymnastics, T-ball, skiing, and visiting cousins in Alabama. Our son was now living in Washington, DC, and our daughter had moved there too, after attending college in Statesboro, Georgia. We shared delightful times in Georgia attending soccer games, for our daughter was blessed to have a soccer scholarship all four years. We would stay at this lovely hotel, Trellis Garden Inn, in a small Georgia town. Oh, did we have fun! We learned about Southern life, boiled peanuts, and grits. Our son would join us sometimes and wonderful family memories were created. We would also meet in Washington, DC, where we enjoyed the children showing us around. Seeing monuments, museums, and trying new restaurants was a great way of getting to know our nation's capital. Walking was our mode of transportation, for the most part.

During one visit, our son pointed out a bicycle, painted all white. It was standing near a pole at an intersection. He explained it was a "ghost bike" placed there to memorialize someone killed riding their bike, and to remind drivers to watch for bicyclists. My daughter, who rode in the Ride of Silence, explained that every year on the third Wednesday in May, people gather in different locations across the world to ride their bicycles in memory of those killed or injured while bicycling.

Ironic that we learned about ghost bikes and the Ride of Silence, for little did we know, we would be participating in such things very soon for someone we loved very, very much!

Chapter Three
July 27th, 2011

*J*uly 27th, 2011, starts out a normal day. My husband Ralph is off to work and I wake up about two hours after he leaves, look out the window, and notice his car is in the driveway. I think, *Hmm, unusual,* as he usually rides to work only one day a week, and had already ridden on Monday. I think that since it is a warm, sunny summer day he must have ridden his bicycle again. It was important to him to ride often to get in the training he needed to participate in a triathlon someday.

I have my usual hot coffee and white creamy yogurt with fresh strawberries, before walking the dog and letting her run in the backyard. I do some chores and head to work about 2:00 pm. I counsel five clients at the nearby psychological clinic that day, and leave at around seven. It has been a gorgeous, sunshiny day. I am so looking forward to getting home and seeing my Ralph. Dinner and talk of the day is one of the best times of the day. We go to a nearby restaurant or Ralph makes something delightful for dinner.

I pull in the drive about 7:10 p.m. and a light rain has begun to fall. I notice the front door closed, which is highly unusual, as our dog Charlie Jo is usually there, looking out and wagging her tail as I approach the door. I think, *Well, maybe he left work late and needs a ride, as it is now raining.* I am also thinking, *Where shall we have dinner? Hmmm, Kerby's Koney*

Island sounds good. I go inside, pet Charlie, and await Ralph's call. The phone does ring at about 7:30, and my life has never been the same since.

"This is Pontiac Osteopathic Hospital calling; your husband has been in an accident; he is unresponsive and bleeding from his head. Are you going to come here?"

I freeze, I cannot breathe, cannot think. *What the hell is this person doing, calling me and stating such mind-blowing crap?* I try to think, try to be normal, try to know what to do next: who to tell, who to call, where to go. I was distraught, it was an incomprehensible moment in time. What do I do with this? I just want Ralph home and a Coney Island hot dog at Kerby's. Now I am not even able to think of names, phone numbers, or anything! I finally recall my sister-in-law's first and last name, then think to find her number on the laptop. I call and share the goddamn incomprehensible message I'd just received. She says she has to get hold of Mike, her husband, and they will be over.

While waiting, I run across the street to Bill, my neighbor. He watches, not knowing what to say, as I pace and wonder out loud if the love of my life is dead. I am feeling scared, nervous and anxious. I call my brother and my children to let them know what has happened and that I am on my way to the hospital. Thunder, lightning, and rain like I have never experienced before surrounds us as we drive through the dark night. I walk into a dark hospital hallway, where a security guard directs us to a barren, bland dark conference room with no Kleenex or water.

Two doctors and two nurses show up. They seat themselves across from the five of us and just stare at us. Yes, just stare at us, no words. It is unbelievable, just fucking unbelievable. No arm around the shoulder, no holding of a hand, no warmth, no compassion! I ask, "Is he dead? Is he dead?" over and over again, for I can no longer stand the silence. The older doctor slowly nods his head. I ask for Kleenex as the shock, dread, and sorrow pours from my eyes. I have to ask for water too. It is a deeply sad and incomprehensible thing to have happen to someone experiencing the death of their beloved. One doctor stated, "These kinds of things happen all the time in the summer." *Gee thanks, that makes me feel better. What the hell?!* They relay the neurologist's comment that my Ralphy would have been a vegetable had he lived. This was also a gut-wrenching thing to say to someone. They never share with me what condition he was in when he arrived at the hospital, what they did, or anything. Almost five years later, I still don't have a clear, precise answer to that lingering question.

They ask someone to identify his body, and suggest that it not be me. My wonderful brother-in-law, an EMS and fireman, volunteers to do it. I ask if I should see him and he says no. I frantically begin calling everyone. I first call my son who is about to begin a vacation in Key West. Dead silence, so deep you could hear a pin drop, when I told him the godforsaken, unbelievable news. I phoned my daughter and the blood curdling scream, "NO!" with heartbreaking tears flowed at me through the line as I told them that the most important man in their life, their father, had just died.

As I write this, I feel the numbness and shock wanting to take over my body, to return as it was that dark, scary night that changed my life. I take a deep breath so as to continue, as I know repeating my story as often as necessary is all part of the grief and healing, whether it is filmmaking, journaling, writing a book, or just talking to a counselor or friend. My story needs to be told over and over again.

Eventually we leave the hospital for Grandma Finneren's condo about 30 miles away to give her the godforsaken, unbelievable news that her only son is dead, killed while riding his bicycle, hit by a distracted driver.

When we arrive, she is sleeping in her chair with the TV on. Shock ensues, we stay for a while, and then I am delivered to my doorstep in Orion Township, Michigan, never to walk through the door with my husband again. Friends begin arriving, food starts rolling in and filling the fridge. People coordinate picking up my son and daughter from airports. The pain of what happened leaves me feeling paralyzed in mind and body.

Judith Finneren

Chapter Four
The Day After

*T*hursday, July 28th, 2011, the day after my life changed forever, I received unexpected phone calls. Oh my God, how I wish someone would have told me what to expect. I remember sitting at the dining room table feeling numb and detached, just going through the motions, when a Channel 2 news reporter called and asked me what kind of husband my Ralph was. I felt shocked, humbled and bewildered. *What?* I thought. "He was a great man, a gentle man, the best husband and father anyone could ask for," I answered. After the phone call, I felt like I could not breathe. Before I could catch my breath, the phone rang again. This time it was the organ donation coordinator. I felt faint and nauseous, also shocked and bewildered again, as I am thinking *Oh, my God, I should not have to be answering this question. Ralph shouldn't be dead!* I answered, "Yes, use what you can." They went on to tell me procedural stuff that I didn't understand. Finishing the phone call, I got up and walked into the kitchen, my stomach empty and my tongue dry. Gazing out the window, gripping the granite counter top until my knuckles turned white, I took a moment to catch my breath and calm down. I returned to the dining room table where my family was busy arranging pictures on poster boards to display at the funeral home. The phone rang again. This time it was the local newspaper, wanting information to do an article. I had had enough phone calls today, so I turned this one over to my son. He chatted a little bit with the compassionate reporter and said he would get back to her later.

My children and I made short videos of his life—a father's, husband's, son's, brother's precious, sweet life. Oh, how does one survive such a barrage of emotions brought on by sitting in a semi-circle in a funeral home to discuss funeral plans or searching the local department store for a dress as if I am going to a fucking party? It was hell, I am telling you. It was hell. I was barely able to move my body as I tried on this pretty black dress. I wore it to the funeral home with a pink, yellow, red and beige scarf to symbolize life, his life, his wonderful, sweet, gentle spirit. His bicycle and banjo sat proudly front and center, embracing our love and sadness. Many people said how they did not know he was involved in so many things.

Afterward, by myself in our living room, I thought I would read the medical and accident reports. I didn't make it past the first couple of pages, as I began feeling sick to my stomach. Reading the words the medical professionals and the sheriff wrote just made me cringe with a depth of agony I had never known. Bad idea, as the horrific, mind-boggling information did not help my grief. Thoughts of the night before began filling my mind; did they do all they could possibly do to save my Ralph's life? That the hospital waited to call an hour after he arrived is unforgivable. In addition to his driver's license, he had his wrist road ID and cell phone ICE (in case of emergency) screen, both of which listed my phone number. Yet, they didn't use any of these to promptly call me. They used his Blue Cross Blue Shield insurance card quite readily, though! Am I bitter and angry over the lack of respect of an immediate phone call to me? Yes, I am. I also asked the sheriff why they did not pick me up at my home, as I was home alone, and hearing that news could have killed me. He responded, "We don't like going on calls like this." Oh, my God, do you believe that this book is non-fiction? Somehow, through the immediate shock and numbness that followed, I remember outrageous and unbelievable pain from the callous, cold, dispassionate words and behaviors of what should have been trained professionals.

Judith Finneren

Chapter Five
Maslow And Chakras

Maslow's Hierarchy of Needs

*W*hat do Maslow's hierarchy of needs[1] and the concept of chakras[2] have to do with grief and healing?

As I was thinking of healing methods to share with you, and learning about chakras at the same time, Maslow's hierarchy of needs came to me. I have always appreciated Maslow's simple, easy-to-understand, pyramid illustration of this concept.

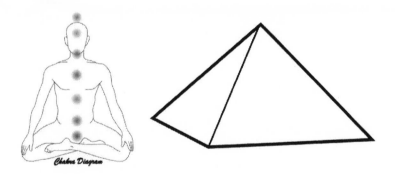

Chakra Diagram

---

[1]McLeod, S. A. 2014. *Maslow's Hierarchy of Needs*. http://www.simplypsychology.org/maslow.html

[2] Devi, Zeffi Shakti. 2014. *From Root to Truth*. [Kindle version]. Retrieved from Amazon.com

Let's start at the bottom with physiological needs. When a person is experiencing grief, their appetite diminishes, and interest in food and water is lessened. They need to be reminded to eat and to drink. Often people bring lots of food to the grieving person's home, hoping they will eat. Others are often seen asking the bereaved if they would like some water. The grieving person needs to be reminded to eat and drink even if she does not feel like it. Usually, shelter is taken care of, as the person does have a place to live, and air is, of course, available. Sexual desire is lessened. Some people who are grieving will have trouble sleeping and some sleep too much. I was blessed to sleep well.

Moving up the pyramid to the next level, we find the need for safety. Feeling safe in one's own home is very important. For me, with my husband gone, I was very aware of people in the neighborhood, knocking on my door, wandering around, or looking suspicious. Unbelievably, some people prey on widows.

Being home alone at night, I would keep more lights on, keep the phone nearby, and listen for our dog's bark. Since my husband was killed by a distracted driver, I also had the intimidating aspect of the law in my life. I had lots of legal involvement with courts, sheriffs, judges, probation officers, and prosecutors. This legal world did not always feel safe to me.

The third level up is huge, and is broken wide open when one experiences the loss of their beloved. This level of the pyramid concerns love and a sense of belonging, specifically friends, family, intimacy, affection, and love. The first and foremost loss experienced is the end of the romantic relationship. For me it was sudden, tragic, and traumatic. In the snap of a finger, that aspect of my life was done. I felt love and caring from friends and family at the outset. However, this wanes as time goes on and the need for love and belongingness increases. As people leave us, we feel isolated, sometimes we feel like something is wrong with us now that our beloved is dead. Sometimes slowly, sometimes suddenly, family and friends return to their own lives and we feel abandoned. As we heal through the grief process and want to be a part of life again, we seek places and people where the need for love and belonging might be met. Twelve-Step programs, churches, meet-ups, Bible study groups, Stephen Ministries, and participating in clubs that have the same interests as we do are some examples. Our workplace may also satisfy some of these needs.

Esteem needs show up second from the top. This involves self-esteem, achievement, mastery, prestige and independence. As we grow developmentally in a life without the loss of our beloved, this need often seems to be met naturally. We attend college, we begin a career, we participate in activities we enjoy, and we feel a sense of achievement and, sometimes, mastery. Sometimes these achievements lead to prestige, admiration from our peers and others. We gain a sense of independence and confidence leading to self-esteem. This is all blown to pieces when someone we love dies. We will get it back again, but for a moment in time, I definitely experienced a loss of independence, for I could not think, focus, remember ... I could barely understand anything at first. Slowly I gained it all back and more. Friends and family helped tremendously with this by being available to listen, sharing activities, encouraging and supporting me in my dreams. This also helped meet the love and belonging needs. Going to film school and now writing this book are means of achievement, mastery, and prestige for me, also meeting self-esteem needs.

The top of the pyramid is self-actualization. This entails awareness of personal potential, self-fulfillment, personal growth, and peak experiences. I believe experiencing the sudden loss of my beloved knocked me head-on into some of the characteristics of a self-actualized person, such as accepting myself and others for who we are, and being more tolerant of uncertainty, more spontaneous in thought and action, more creative, and more deeply appreciative of basic life experience. I believe those of us who have lost a person in our lives whom we deeply loved, appreciate life so much more than those who have not lost a loved one—we want to live life and experience as much as we can, for we understand how precious this gift of life is. Each breath is a breath of gratitude.

We are basically starting over from the bottom of the pyramid when we experience a deep loss. No wonder grief is a major adjustment.

Chakras

Where do chakras come in?

Chakras are energy centers located throughout our bodies that affect our health, emotions, and spiritual states. Our chakras become misaligned and closed when we are experiencing deep grief. If these energy centers stay out of sync with our health, we may end up with disease. Dis-ease means "not at ease" with ourselves or with life. Our physical and psychological balance is disturbed when we experience the loss of a loved one. Understanding and clearing the chakras is an aid in healing always, but especially during grief. Let us now look at information specifically related to each chakra.

The first chakra, located at the base of the spine, is the root chakra. It is associated with the color red and the element earth. Mother Earth provides us with our survival needs, such as food, clothing, and shelter. When all is well with this chakra and the energy is flowing freely, we feel at home, safe and secure in the world. We are able to stand up for ourselves as well as provide for ourselves. In a very similar fashion, Maslow describes the characteristics in the first two levels of the pyramid, leading to the top, which is self-actualization. So, the first two levels of the pyramid relate to the first chakra.

The sacral chakra, located in the lower abdomen, is associated with the color orange. When this chakra is healthy, we feel peaceful and content with ourselves and the world. We are patient, nurturing and secure. We are comfortable in our own skin. We are able to communicate clearly, and trust our gut instincts. A feeling of intimacy is shared with our friends, family, community and planet. If this chakra's energy is healthy and flowing freely, the process of making healthy changes happens easily. Love and belonging, the third level up in Maslow's pyramid, relate to this second chakra.

The solar plexus chakra is located right in the center of the torso and is associated with the color yellow. It has the potential to raise consciousness and self-awareness. It is governed by fire and is action-oriented. When this energy center is flowing freely, it brings spontaneity, energy, and effectiveness. This energy center resonates with a strong sense of self, integrity, and self-discipline. The third chakra

27

corresponds to the fourth level of Maslow's pyramid, which is related to self-esteem.

The heart chakra is associated with the color green, which represents growth and healing. The color of love, rose, is also associated with this chakra. The heart chakra is the balance point between your physical reality and your spiritual reality. The three chakras below it are physical and the three above are spiritual. The heart chakra is the center of the energy system, where emotions are balanced. If this chakra is blocked, balancing may be difficult, due to the inability of energy to flow freely between the physical and spiritual bodies. When the heart chakra is healed, giving and receiving love is felt instinctively and one feels balanced in heart, mind, body, and soul. Personal growth and fulfillment relates to the top of Maslow's pyramid: self-actualization. Our heart chakra is affected very deeply during grief and loss.

When our heart chakra is closed down, the very core of us suffers. Our breathing is shallow, which slows down our metabolism and our physical energy. We may withdraw from the world. Indeed some days we do just that, especially immediately after the death. Self-love and loving others needs to be balanced and interconnected. Love teaches us to let go, and let God. When our fourth chakra is healed and healthy, we have a feeling of oneness with all that is, and experience grace.

The spiritual fifth, sixth and seventh chakras relate to what Maslow later described as self-transcendence. Once our physiological, safety, love/belongingness and self-esteem needs are met we are motivated to reach our full potential through spiritual growth. The fifth chakra, the throat chakra, relates to speaking our truth and using our voice. It is about becoming one with all that is vibrating around us. The color associated with this chakra is turquoise. It is about communication with self, with spirit and the expression of feelings. In grief, sometimes we do not express our intense pain and sorrow. We do not know who to speak to, or who will understand us. This can lead to a closed chakra, the blockage of the expression of who we truly are. Especially with grief, we need to speak it, write it, share it, express it creatively and release it, thereby keeping our throat and heart chakras open. This leads to the health of our whole being. Suppressing feelings may lead to abuse of food, tobacco, drugs, or alcohol. During grief, we may experience any of these. When the throat chakra is open, energy flowing freely, it is easy to communicate and be understood. Our voice is full. Problems and difficult situations are easily managed, as we are in a state of acceptance. We are inspired to express our higher self, our spiritual self, and we feel strong physically and psychologically. Truthful communication and intimacy fill our lives with wonderful nurturing and loving relationships. Again, we are in a state of oneness with all that is.

The sixth chakra is also known as the "third eye." It is located in the center of the forehead, just above the brow line. It is associated with the color blue. When our third eye is open and energy is flowing freely, we want to know a higher truth, have spiritual perceptions, insights, intuition, and inspiration. We are unafraid to see the truth in our life. When our sixth chakra is open, our higher senses are activated and our perceptions of life will expand. Our ability to connect with our beloved on the other side is a real possibility. I was sharing with a new friend how I seem to connect quite often with my deceased husband while I am driving my car. He seems to be in the passenger seat and I just feel his presence. It is always a healing, loving experience. It is the last car he bought for me, in 2007. My friend shared that she knows people who get messages from things, like feathers, pennies, cardinals, etc. She would like to dream or communicate in some way with her deceased mother. She spoke of never experiencing any type of communication with her mother. I am wondering if energy work on opening her third eye would help her experience communication with her mother? We truly have to let go and let God. We need to open our spiritual wings, our third eye, and our heart chakra and believe that our loved ones will communicate with us. When it happens, there is no doubt it was them and we feel comforted.

The seventh chakra, the "crown" chakra, is indigo-colored and located on the top of the head. It is the center for our highest spiritual consciousness. It transcends all the senses and focuses on the spiritual meaning of life. When it is open, we take in greater knowledge and wisdom that lies beyond the level of the physical body. We live in the now moment. One feels faithful, joyful, at peace, and grateful. On a physical level, one is energetic and full of life no matter what the biological age. Direct oneness and communion with spirit is achieved. When it is closed, one feels disconnected from spirit, alone and separate. Fear, shame, and depression may rise. Disease may occur. An inability to live in the present may take place. One may always be concerned about the future or stuck in the past.

We should seek to always have balanced chakras, especially after a devastating loss. Maslow's hierarchy of needs shows us physically and psychologically the path necessary to reach self-actualization, to satisfy a need within us all, while balancing the chakras helps us to live a healthy life, while connecting with the divine. Several methods exist to balance chakras, such as affirmations, meditation, journaling, dancing, and classes. When I looked at Maslow's hierarchy of needs and the need for our chakras to be balanced, I understood more than ever why we feel so crappy after the loss of a loved one. With understanding came compassion for myself and my grieving process.

Judith Finneren

Chapter Six
Ghost Bike

I am not sure exactly when we placed the ghost bike, but it was just days after the moment that changed our lives forever. My two children and I chose one of two matching bicycles that had been hanging in the rafters of the garage. They were the bicycles used when the children were little, some twenty years ago. We would ride on the wonderful bike path at Stoney Creek Metro Park. Sometimes the then four-year-old would cry and off Ralph would go, faster and faster, until our son delighted in the speed through his tears. It seemed to work for both children. We rode our bicycles all over. Sometimes we rode at Indian Springs Metro Park too, even as the children got old enough to ride their own bicycles, riding a variety of places to exercise and nurture their connection to the wonders of nature. To this day, they both love riding bikes. The Paint Creek Trail and the Polly Ann Trail were two of our favorites, as we could just hop on those from home. We also rode the "big loop" and the "little loop" as our family named them, paths in our neighborhood. Oh, what fun we had! We timed ride competitions with each other and held Finneren duathlons.

I got carried away in sweet memories. We painted our ghost bike white and placed it on Giddings Road, north of Brown Road at the scene of the crash as a memorial; a reminder to motorists to be mindful of bicyclists, and a reminder to us all of how precious and fragile this gift of life is.

I have had several friends tell me they think of me and Ralph and say a little prayer every time they pass by. I am so grateful for the gift of others' thoughts and prayers.

The Guardian, a British national daily newspaper, states that the first recorded ghost bike was in St. Louis, Missouri, in 2003. A person witnessed a collision between a motorist and a bicyclist and placed a white painted bicycle at the location with a sign that read: "Cyclist struck here." Currently, over 630 ghost bikes have appeared in over 210 locations around the world.

Judith Finneren

Chapter Seven
The Path Of Love

The path of love during grief is also useful in everyday life. The path of love is different for each individual. It involves connecting with Source. Source can be anything, as long as it is a power greater than oneself. My source is God and Mother Nature. Churches, twelve-step programs, talking with loved ones, walking, and spending time near bodies of water are all great ways of connecting with the divine spark within us all.

Sharing our stories brings healing and hope to both ourselves and others. The path of love is always available to us, though sometimes we find ourselves veering off course. That is OK, we just get back on. God forgives us and blesses us even when we are off-course. We will find our way back to intimacy with God, self, and others. Intimacy or "into-me-see," means letting others in, letting them help us, or asking for help. It means having honest, deep conversations without masks or false self—just us—pure, innocent, and precious as the day we arrived on the planet, just the way God made us. When someone we love dies, we go back to that basic self, in all our rawness and vulnerability. It is amazing! To stay in that place and grow presents a new challenge, for others are surprised by how different we are now. We have to let go of some people who don't understand, people who before the loss might have been close family members or friends. We grow as we stay in our innocence and purity. The world tries to pull us back in and, with awareness, we don't let that happen. Most of us who have experienced a gut-wrenching, horrific loss no longer take this precious gift of life for granted. I was reading this morning some comments on a widows/widowers' website that was discussing the issue of feeling alone and isolated. Someone mentioned that it is us who feel differently, like we don't fit in anymore. Mentioned often is the pain of friends and family not calling, not coming around, as if we widows/widowers are diseased.

When I first had these feelings, I thought it was just me. I thought I was not handling grief well; I was not coping. It felt so good to know that I was not alone in these feelings. People do leave us! The truth is plain and simple: people do not know what to say; they are afraid we will burst into unstoppable tears. They are afraid to feel what we may be feeling, knowing that it will happen to them or their spouse one day. When they look at us, they are reminded of the depth of sorrow that occurs with the loss of a beloved. The truth is, if they would really empathize with us, as best they can, the ability to help us, just sit with us, be with us, would grow stronger. A lady I had just met in the church fellowship hall after the Sunday service said to my widower friend and myself, touching my arm, looking at both our faces, "I am so sorry for your broken hearts, and I am so happy for you guys and the happiness you found." That is one of the most profound things anybody has ever said to us. She acknowledged the losses and validated our new lives. It was wonderful!

Judith and Ralph enjoying a cruise celebrating thirty fifth
wedding anniversary.

Judith, Ralph, Rory and Holli. Family wedding 2009.

Ralph and Charlie Jo at Lumberman's Monument, Oscoda, MI.

Holli, Judith, Rory and Ralph
"Best family ever---ok I'm prejudiced" Ralph Finneren

Ralph and Judith

Ralph, Judith, Holli and Rory at Holli's graduation from
Georgia Southern 2009.

Ralph in his first duathlon, Lake Orion, MI.

Ralph, Holli and Rory, Lake Orion, MI.

Sailing was a favorite pastime.

Judith and Charlie Jo relaxing in northern Michigan.

Judith Finneren

Chapter Eight
Film School

Film school played a major role in my healing. Fall of 2012, beginning of August, I began my journey from Lake Orion, Michigan, to Sedona, Arizona, to attend the Zaki Gordon Institute for Independent Filmmaking. I had made the decision about a year prior, only three months post-trauma, to attend film school the following fall. I had attended an orientation there, and Spirit led me to say yes. So with excitement, fear, joy, and anticipation in my heart of experiencing a new way of life for a while, we prepared for the road.

My sister-in-law, my wonderful, loving, canine companion Charlie Jo, and I all packed in my Pontiac G-5! What a sight we were, suitcases and bags packed to the roof. I chuckle now to think of how packed that car was. We had car problems from the very beginning. Before we even got out of Detroit, the car overheated due to the air-conditioning running. After exiting at a run-down area with boarded up buildings in Detroit, where there was no auto repair facility to be seen, we hurried back on the highway for a more welcoming exit farther up the road. We found an auto repair shop, they helped us out, and off we went. We stopped every couple of hours to stretch our legs, use the bathroom, get a bite to eat, and let the dog out. CJ loved to travel and lay quietly in the back seat, usually not making a peep. But one time as we were driving, she suddenly popped up between the two of us in the front seats and started making the strangest guttural sounds. "Oh no!" I said to my sister-in-law who was driving, "Pull over—she is going to puke!" The nearest area to pull over was a truck weigh station. It wasn't open, thank goodness, so we pulled in and got her out. We giggled as Charlie Jo took care of business while I cleaned myself up a bit as a little had gotten on my jeans. It only happened that one time on our six-day, five-night journey. We stayed in different hotels, enjoyed dining at local mom-and-pop restaurants with occasional stops at Starbucks. Arriving in northern Arizona, we spotted the signs for the Painted Desert and Petrified Forest. We made short quick stops at both as Charlie Jo did not have a lot of patience for such things. At the Painted Desert the colors of the sands and rocks mesmerized us with brilliant shades of red, oranges and lavenders. At the Petrified Forest the colors of the wood turned into stone fascinated us as our eyes gazed upon the beauty. I don't remember much else about the journey from Michigan to Arizona, or my old life to my new life, as this trip occurred only one year and a few days after losing my Ralph. I was with it enough to do things in the present moment, but still not one hundred percent in thought, memory and emotion. My brain and body were able to function while slowly healing, becoming unthawed and out of paralysis from the sudden tragedy that occurred only months before. This journey was so much more than driving in a car from Michigan to Arizona. It was a journey from my "old normal," to what would become my "new normal." What a wonderful journey it was, and what a great feeling to pull into the driveway at my rental home in Sedona a few days later.

I met a couple of neighbors and felt at home immediately. I was familiar with Sedona, having visited it every year since 2006. Finally, I was going to live here for a while. It was a dream come true, to live in Sedona! I was right where I needed to be, and I knew it. One of my neighbors is still a close friend of mine. She lived in a garage that had been converted to a studio apartment, right next door. It made me feel safe and not so alone once my sister-in-law had gone back, and it did help with learning to live alone.

I bought a local newspaper soon after arriving, and what should I see, but an article about the Zaki Gordon Institute for Independent Filmmaking closing? *This is why I am here,* I thought. *What's going on?* I began to panic, but after reading the article further and seeing an email from the head of the film school, I understood the school wasn't closing, only that they were changing their name to Sedona Film School. With that, my nerves calmed down and I felt better.

My sister-in-law stayed a few nights, helping me get settled in. Some friends recommended I get a house blessing and knew just the right person to do that. I contacted her and before you knew it, a gathering and Native American house-blessing ceremony took place in my home. Oh, what fun! This was a new experience for me, too! My thoughtful friends surprised me with a mirror, on the frame of which they had all written personal notes. I hung it with pride in the vestibule of my new temporary home. It would be my home for the next several months, and that mirror would remind me daily of my friends' love and support. I was grateful and humbled.

Right before the official start of the house blessing, when all of us were gathered in the living room, I heard a strange gurgling noise coming from the bathroom. I arose to check it out, and spraying upwards from the toilet, as if a fountain of glory, was a water blessing. It was all over the floor and dampening the carpet in the hallway. I called the landlord and he came over immediately. It makes me laugh and smile now. What amazing timing! Water has always been a healing force in my life, so I saw it as a blessing. I was not expecting it to show itself like that!

In film school I created *Ghostbike*, a twenty-minute short documentary of tragedy, forgiveness, healing, and hope. One of my motivations for going to film school was wanting to transform the pain of losing my husband into something creative. Another deciding factor was that I had just found out in the previous couple of years that I have a passion for filmmaking. I was exposed to the process as an extra in a couple of films made in my home state of Michigan.

So began a journey of healing and hope as the film was being created. I had classes five days a week, Monday through Friday -- sometimes Saturday and Sunday, too. I loved it! I met lots of wonderful, compassionate folks. I was a fifty-six-year-old woman among mostly men in their twenties and a few other women who all helped me so much. I am thankful to this day for all my classmates and instructors. Not only did they help me create a lasting legacy for my beloved, they lifted my spirits, gave me something to focus on, and something new to learn. When I got stuck and had difficulty understanding something, one of my classmates was always there and kind enough to help me. It was a fantastic experience!

We began using the equipment immediately. The instructor oriented us to the camera, tripod, and microphones and taught us how to produce and direct. For the first four months, we worked in small groups, taking turns being producer, director, camera person, and audio technician. Each week we chose a different topic. We had to pitch our topic to the class, and then the class voted on which one we would do. We filmed shorts of five minutes or less. We went all over Sedona, Flagstaff and other nearby cities filming. Sometimes when I think about this and remember all the learning and work I did, I don't know how I did it. Then I remember it was God—it was Spirit—that led me to Sedona and film school at that time and with those people.

The last four months from January to May was the making of our thesis film. We wrote and directed this film, asking classmates and others to be our producers, camera, and audio. We had to write a script and have it approved by our instructors. One of our classes involved learning about fundraising using the Internet. I was sitting home one night with Charlie Jo, my canine companion, and I thought, *Heck, I don't know anything about it, but I shall try*. I decided to apply what I had learned in the fundraising class. Before I knew it, I had set up an Indiegogo site. I raised $5,000. It covered flights to Michigan, hotels, and food for my crew.

We made it to Michigan and my home, where I had not been in seven months. I had two people checking on it, with hopes that all would be clean and well taken care of for me and my crew. Well, there were mouse turds in the family room, on the fireplace mantel. My audio guy was very nice and offered to clean them up for us. Thank you, Jerod! We had a fun night playing games when suddenly Jerod spotted my old guitar and asked if he could play it. We sang the night away.

The next day, my children arrived. It was hard emotionally for them to come home and see cameras, lights, and three strangers in their home. We went for a car ride to discuss privately and decided to ask the crew to move to a hotel, paid for by me, of course. Once the emotional level decreased a little, all was well. The children were OK to be interviewed, and shared touching thoughts. It was difficult for me too—lots of tears! Then, lots of love and hugs followed. We interviewed the sheriff who was in charge of the case, a witness of the accident, and then took some shots of the ghost bike with the crew. The crew was so creative; they went out to different bicycle shops and got some good B-roll (supplemental shots for context, setting, and transition) for the film. I was so proud of them! I got to show them some of the places we enjoyed as a family in our hometown. Lake Orion was one, though it was completely frozen over as it was winter time. They loved it and slid all over the place on the ice, laughing and giggling, as they were not used to ice and snow, being from Arizona.

We eventually headed back to Sedona. I was blessed to have an amazing film editor. I want to share with you the synchronicity of how we met. I was honored to have a poem I wrote published in a local Sedona poetry book. I was attending the book-release party at a private home. It was a gorgeous home with a huge fireplace, and I met a lot of new folks. I was sitting on the lower fireplace ledge, enjoying some delicious food, and I began chatting with a lady. I mentioned to her that I was creating a film and in search of an editor. I had already spoken with a couple of others and had no luck. She immediately replied, "I know a perfect person for you—here is her number." *Wow,* I thought, *this is amazing.* I phoned the editor soon thereafter, and we met at a local restaurant for lunch. She agreed to be my editor. I was again so very blessed, as she did a fantastic job. *Ghostbike*, my twenty-minute short documentary, was completed May, 2013. It has been shown in several film festivals and private screenings. I am so proud of it and of myself for accomplishing this goal. It was a healing journey and part of my hope-after-loss experience. It is a journey that I am so thankful for.

I believe life is a tapestry of synchronicities. We sometimes do not notice the synchronicity right away. It may take days, months, or years to notice. We also do not see immediately how the synchronicities are woven together. Then we experience an "Aha!" moment, and things that were confusing start to make a little more sense.

Chapter Nine
Ride Of Silence

*T*he annual Ride of Silence plays a huge role in my healing journey also. It is on the third Wednesday of May every year at 7:00 p.m. Eastern Daylight Time. It takes place around the world to honor those injured or killed while riding their bicycles. It also aims to raise awareness among motorists, city officials, police, and the public that bicyclists have a legal right to the public roadways. Bicyclists gather about an hour before the ride, the names of those killed are read, rules of the ride (such as riding single file, in silence, with a helmet) are discussed, and then off the silent bicyclists go. It is awe-inspiring. I have ridden every year since Ralph's death except 2014, when I filmed it. People in the streets stare at us as we ride in silent procession, wondering what we are doing. We do not speak as we hand them brochures explaining the event. It is an honor to ride for those killed or injured—bicyclists knowing someone who was killed don a black armband and those who have been injured or know someone who has been injured wear a red armband.

My first Ride of Silence, in 2012, was really, really difficult. It was close to ten months after the tragedy, the loss of my love of thirty-seven years. My daughter rode also, as well as friends and other family members. My mother-in-law did not ride a bike, but was there to honor and show respect to her son. As I heard "Ralph Finneren, killed in Orion Township,

July 27, 2011," tears rolled down my cheeks. It was real and here we were, honoring my husband, my children's father. My daughter and I hugged side-by-side in a loving embrace, sharing the deep feelings of pain and loss. Then we all rode in silent procession. It felt so good, to have so much love and support. By the end, returning back, and gathering for the final time that night, people began taking pictures as true, heartfelt smiles came across our faces. We had honored a man who was deeply loved, treasured, and missed.

The Ride of Silence began in Dallas in 2003 after a man was hit and killed. A friend of this man, Chris Phelan, started the initiative, thinking it would be a one-time event. Chris sent out emails and word-of-mouth brought 1,000 cyclists to that first Ride of Silence. Media coverage reported motorists and people on the street stopping, knowing something special was happening—a statement was being made. Pats on the back, tears being shed, a camaraderie of bicyclists honoring and riding in memory of those killed or injured. Those killed or injured were someone's husband, son, father, wife, daughter, mother, or friend—a precious human life taken, or a life changed forever. This Ride of Silence was to honor them and increase awareness for all to drive mindfully. I read the following poem at every Ride of Silence I participate in, and tears roll down my cheeks every time:

The Ride of Silence

Tonight we number many but ride as one
In honor of those not with us, friends, mothers, fathers, sisters, sons
With helmets on tight and heads down low,
We ride in silence, cautious and slow
The wheels start spinning in the lead pack

But tonight, we ride and no one attacks
The dark sunglasses cover our tears
Remembering those we held so dear
Tonight's ride is to make others aware
The road is there for all to share
To those not with us or by our side,
May God be your partner on your final ride.
- Mike Murgas

Chapter Ten
Back To Life

We must take very good care of ourselves during this period of grief, as illness and disease may creep in. I remember my friend Enocha from Your Heart's Home near Sedona, Arizona, reminding me to keep my heart and mind open during this period. At times, it was super hard; I just wanted to shut down and curl up in a ball. "Don't you dare give up," was another bit of advice I received from a close friend. Sometimes it feels like your whole world has gone black, motionless, emotionless, dead; as if we died with the person we are grieving. A part of us will forever be changed. We need to remember that we are alive, breathing, living, loving and still a part of this precious life here on earth. We are in fact honoring our loved one who is no longer here by continuing to participate in this gift of life. That is definitely what they would want. One takes baby steps for sure some days. This will not come all at once, but in time we will experience laughter, joy, and the precious gifts of life again.

My Process and Synchronicities

It was the middle of September when my friend went back home to Pennsylvania after so generously living with me for six weeks after Ralph's death. She stayed with me through mood swings, tons of tears and all the stuff that creates deep grief. She and another friend helped me handle paper work that my brain just could not handle at the time. I am so grateful.

A typical week for me after my friend's six-week visit looked like this:

- 8:00 a.m.: Wake up, meditate, pray, and journal. Check e-mails, Facebook, and other interesting things online. Let the dog out back.
- 9:30 a.m. – 10:30a.m.: On Mondays, Wednesdays, and Fridays, workout at the gym. On Thursdays, go to yoga at the Methodist church.
- 11:00a.m. – noon: Attend a spiritual gathering or attend Bible study for an hour.
- Noon – 2:00 p.m.: Lunch.
- 2:00 p.m.: Arrive back home and ask myself, *Now what?*
- 5:00 p.m.: On Monday evenings, my Stephen Minister would arrive, which I so looked forward to. On Tuesdays, sometimes a friend would visit.

I needed all the support and help I could get during this intense grief period. My neighbor invited me to a Bible study at her church. If you knew me, you would know that I am not a Bible person. I have faith, and believe in God, but I don't go around quoting the Bible as the be-all and end-all, nor do I care to listen to people who do. Never would I have dreamed of going to a Bible study. When she invited me, I asked, "What time?" She pulled into my driveway the following Tuesday, we picked up a neighbor from around the block, and off we went.

What a delightful group of women! We read a passage from the Bible, answered questions, and discussed the passage and what it meant to us in our lives. Everyone was so loving, kind, and understanding. God placed these angels in my life, right when I needed them. Thank you, Jesus. We went to lunch afterword, which was also so needed. I was still pretty numb, pretty out of it, so I appreciated any help I could get, where people would literally pick me up, and drop me off. It was very hard to initiate things, as my mind and body were still in shock. This all took place in the months following the tragedy. I am so grateful for these ladies and the time they took to love me, share with me, and talk with me. Even the waitress at the restaurant lit up my day.

At some point, I signed up with the local Methodist church to have a Stephen Minister visit with me weekly. I had seen the words "Stephen Minister" before and really never paid much attention or knew what that meant. Well, the program teaches laypersons to provide one-on-one care for individuals who request support. So a person wanting to be a Stephen Minister gets trained on how to counsel people in their time of need. Reasons may be divorce, major illness, addictions, or other types of grief or loss. The relationship may last weeks to years. The Stephen Minister grows spiritually and psychologically as they help others. I had a delightful relationship with a woman who was my Stephen Minister. She visited every Monday evening, and I so looked forward to that visit. She stayed one or two hours. Again, another angel was placed on my healing path. Thank you, God.

Having no one to share with, I felt like I had nothing to do at home. I had plenty to do—sort through my husband's clothes and personal items—but I just did not feel like it yet. Stuff around the house sat the same way it was the moment I got the devastating call, as if my life was on "pause." I, too, was paused, sitting the same way, in the same spot on the couch in the corner, with sticky notes plastered all over the side of the fireplace, sticky notes with phone numbers and names of people who suggested I call them, if needed. What they did not understand, although it was very nice of them to offer, was that I did not have the gumption, the get-up-and-go, the motivation, or energy to call them. I needed them to call me, to tell me that they would come and pick me up to go to lunch, or tell me they were coming over at a certain time.

At times, when I was feeling a little more will to live, I would call. But sometimes you just want to die when the love of your life has died. I felt that way often in the first year. I tried to plan at least a week ahead to fill gaps in my calendar with some activity. I would shop sometimes, see a friend for lunch, or we'd visit at their home or mine. It is really, really difficult getting used to not talking to that one special person in your life and going home to a dead house that was once filled with life. Some Saturdays there were invitations to special events or friends' children's sporting events, but Saturdays were probably the most difficult, as I usually had no plans despite my efforts to stay busy.

I felt like a robot, like a part of me had died, too. I attended events just to be with people and feel alive. I also went to three different therapists for a while. I felt so lonely and so hopeless sitting home alone. My son and daughter visited often that first year. That was a godsend. My son was able to work here in Michigan as well as in DC; what a gift that was. He offered to come as often as he could. My daughter, that first year of grief, was very busy in her last year of graduate school, working on her degree. She graduated in the spring of 2012 and, boy, was that a mixed bag of emotions. I know Ralph was there in spirit, for I felt his warmth, but, oh, did it ache that he was not there in physical form, holding my hand and seeing his daughter graduate with a doctorate in physical therapy.

I had four people who welcomed me to spend the night if need be. I stayed at one friend's home about four nights, and the other, a couple of nights. It helped a lot. I am so thankful. It gave me a nice break from sitting home alone. It was nice to know that the option was available.

GriefShare, a program a lot of churches offer, also was a part of my healing and growth after loss. A group of grieving people and I met weekly for about six weeks. We watched a video, then answered questions and discussed where we were in the grief process. It was very helpful.

The first fellow widow I ever encountered was a gal I met online through a common acquaintance. She and some friends from work were meeting for dinner, and she invited me along. I had a wonderful time. It felt so good to chat with someone who really understood. Chatting about widowhood and life made me feel not so alone. We are still friends and chat every now and then.

I joined a few meetup groups as I began feeling better. I only made it to a couple of gatherings, which I enjoyed very, very much. One was a jazz concert dinner, held outdoors on a warm summer evening. As I got healthier, more motivated, and wanting to be a part of life again, my life and calendar filled up naturally. I did not have to try to make it happen. What a great feeling! The other meetup was about creating films, which I loved. I attended that one a few times.

While living in Sedona attending film school, I walked Charlie Jo down the street every day, sometimes many times a day. After doing this for about a month, I decided to stop and read a sign I had never paid attention to before. It displayed the name and number of a therapist—a grief and loss specialist. I stood there in absolute awe. This house with the sign was two doors away from my home. Charlie Jo and I finished our walk, and I phoned. I set up an appointment and felt so blessed.

The synchronicity of these events amazes me. I believe someone is hearing us and knows what we need. I believe it to be God, Spirit, blessed Mother, guardian angels, or archangels.

My healing journey was taking on so many sweet aspects: new people, new activities, and a renewed sense of self. I saw this amazing woman several times and gained insights I needed. God and Spirit were taking excellent care of me, and I knew it. I knew it because I didn't have to think or make decisions. Gifts were placed before me, and I knew on a deep heartfelt level what I needed to do. It felt right.

At one visit, I mentioned my back was bothering me. I recently had helped a friend move some furniture, and I was feeling it. The therapist explained that she'd had back problems and acupuncture had really helped her. I said I was willing to try it. She shared with me a phone number of a local acupuncturist, and I set up my first appointment. I was open and willing, but a little hesitant to have someone start sticking needles in me. Much to my surprise, I loved it! I have been getting acupuncture for about four years now.

I also often got massages at Your Heart's Home, from Enocha, whom I had met the first time I went to Sedona. Her home in Oak Creek Canyon is in a secluded area north of uptown Sedona, with the pristine Oak Creek running through it. I found Oak Creek to be a huge blessing in my life. My friend is not only a massage therapist; she is a healer, and she works in many traditions, including Native American, shamanic, and others. At one of my sessions, we walked to the creek, and I released lots of negativity to the water. I fell in love with the water. I visited it often, as I love the sound of water rippling over the rocks, the mini-waterfalls, and the luscious sights and smells. Oak Creek became healing ground for me.

Martha, my neighbor whom I was blessed to become friends with, is a dancer. I had arrived in Sedona August of 2012 and in October, Martha was doing an outdoor Halloween dance in uptown Sedona. She was holding practices for six weeks prior and asked me to join in. I was like, "I can't dance—I am not a dancer." We drove together several times to the studio where practices were being held. I loved it. I was trying something new, stepping outside of my comfort zone, and enjoying. I was tasting life again in new ways.

Drumming became another activity I enjoyed, as the rhythm of drumbeats was such an ancient healing sound to me. Some new friends invited me to attend a drumming session at a local bar. At eight in the evening, they move the tables to create space for a drummer semi-circle, dancers in the center. I was enchanted and mesmerized. Mostly I drummed, but I danced a few times and listened a few times. Each healing event lasted a couple of hours. Sometimes the drumming got a little too intense for me, and I would leave after an hour, feeling peaceful and complete. Even now as I am remembering and transcribing all the ways that healing took place for me, I am amazed and thrilled at God's grace.

I remember a couple of really lonely depressing times while in Sedona. Both times I went to the natural food store to pick up groceries and, lo and behold, both times I ran into the same two people. It felt so good, synchronistic, and was what I needed to break through the feelings of despair. I was not alone. I was being taken care of by powers outside of myself.

For the most part I was able to keep my heart and mind open during the grief process, and amazing things happened and continue to happen as long as I stay open-hearted and -minded. As I am grateful, I realize I am given more to be grateful for. One of the hardest and most powerful things I did was come up with this affirmation: "I am so thankful for the times we were given to share. Thank you blessed Mother-Father God, spirit guides, and guardian angels." So I developed, over time, a spirit of gratitude for the time Ralph and I were given to be in each other's lives and to create two loving human beings who are pure gifts to this world. This way, I was focusing on what I had, not what I had lost. I was told by several people that I was blessed to have loved and been loved, for some people never experience this. I do not take this love for granted. It is a true gift and I am humbled.

Sedona Soul Adventure

I must share with you a story from 2006, during my first trip to Sedona. I did what they call a soul adventure, in which I visited five or six different healers. As I approached one healer's home, I noticed a dome shape in the distance. I have always admired dome-shaped homes. I was super excited and a little nervous.

I approached the door and was greeted by a Native American in full regalia. *Wow. Beautiful,* I thought. *Awesome.* He suggested I be seated and he sat down also. After we introduced ourselves, he smudged the area using a feather, sage, and sweet grass. I love the smell of sage and sweet grass.

Smudging is a ritual that is used for cleansing, clearing, and inviting blessings to a space or person. Sage helps clear negative energies. Once a sacred space has been cleared, the sweet grass is used to call in good spirits, encourage wellness, and create a tone of positive influences. It was awesome and familiar to me, as I had experienced smudging several times before with various groups and at a sweat lodge I had attended several years prior.

We chatted for a while and then went for a walk through the neighborhood and into the red rocks among agave plants, cacti, and trees. We walked quietly, and upon entering the nature space from the neighborhood, he taught me to honor the four directions, turning my body in a circle. He said we should do this always when entering and exiting a natural space. I remembered and did just that for a few years. What stands out most to me is when we stopped at an agave plant and he told me to pull a leaf up that I felt a connection to. If it was too hard to pull up, I was to let it go and find another. I believe it was on my second try that I was able to pull the leaf up and away, severing its connection to the main plant. He then had me peel strings off its side. I was thinking, *Interesting. Hmmm.* He then asked that I braid them, and told me that I was creating a life bracelet. When I was done, he would "read" it to me. I remember feeling very much in the zone, in the spirit world, when I began braiding the agave. At one point, I jumped. When he asked, "What?" I said, "I don't know. I heard something, but I thought it was you." It was not him; he was very quiet the whole time and had not moved. I am not sure, to this day, what it was. Spirit? I finished the braid and the healer said, "There will come a time in your life when you will feel very, very alone. Please remember you are never alone, for Great Spirit is always with you." I have remembered those precious words, so needed, during my grief journey. Again, I have so much gratitude for this wisdom that was especially needed in 2011. I'm amazed by this tapestry of life, the synchronicities of life unfolding, as we keep our hearts and minds open.

Unity of Sedona:

Unity of Sedona, a magnificent spiritual center, also boosted my healing process. I met the spiritual leader, Michael Mirdad, about three months after Ralph's death. After one of the Sunday services, I told him of the tragedy as tears streamed down my cheeks. As if he were an angel placed on my path, he said, "Let his body go, and take in his spirit." It helps me to remember those wise words. They are comforting words of healing, hope, and inspiration. They have helped me understand that my beloved, my Ralph, is always with me and is a part of me. I then had a little healing ceremony done by one of the chaplains. I so love that, at this unique spiritual center, you can get a healing done after each service on Sundays.

When I lived in Sedona for ten months while making my first film, I attended the spiritual center regularly. It filled me with love, hope, and joy. It helped me so much, as did so many of the other angels I have previously mentioned that God put before me. Lunch in the fellowship hall after the noon service was a great time to chat with other people. Feeling connected to others and to life is so important as one walks in grief's footsteps.

About a year after my initial talk with Michael, I felt the need to make an appointment with him. He offered counseling sessions. I spoke to Michael again of my recent tragedy. I liked him; I trusted him and knew I would get the help I needed. I reminded him of who I was and what happened in my life. We chatted a little bit, and then he stood, walked over by me, and said, "You will experience a miracle today." I had my eyes closed, and a few seconds later, water was dripping down my cheek, just a single drop. I was thinking, is that Jesus' tear, letting me know he feels the depth of my sorrow? After sitting in silence for a bit, feeling as if I experienced a true miracle, and thinking the session was over, I heard Michael say, hang on to me. I rose from the chair and in a heavenly embrace of pure empathy, of and through God, I sobbed and sobbed, letting it all out, releasing stored pain. Whew! I felt better and I left there renewed in mind, body, and spirit. I thank Michael and Unity of Sedona for the healing it provided me at such a necessary time in my life. I am feeling so blessed today, having attended Unity from October through March, 2015-2016.

The miracles just keep coming. My life is full of them, as long as I keep my heart and mind open. I am also grateful for the peace, love, joy, gratitude, and abundance I experience each and every day. Lastly, while attending Unity during film school, I met a lovely gentleman who invited me to hike with him. We hiked several times during this period. It was fun and we enjoyed several delightful conversations as we shared each other's company among the stunning red rocks of Sedona! I was coming back to life.

Judith Finneren

Chapter Eleven
Secondary Losses

*O*h my God, I'm living alone, now, after thirty-seven years of marriage. Are you kidding me? How am I going to do this? I felt so scared—petrified, even. Being totally alone for the first time in my life, I discovered secondary losses, the unexpected challenges of the grief journey. I will share as many as I remember so you are not caught off guard.

First, let me describe the primary loss. This is the actual loss of the loved one from our lives. For me that happened in steps. I first felt excruciating pain and sorrow. Tears and gut-wrenching pain that words will never be able to describe. I then, at some point, realized the pain of my husband Ralph losing his own life. He lost his life. He no longer is breathing, will not walk his daughter down the aisle at her wedding, will not be a grandpa, will never ride a bicycle again, or sail with his son. His life has ended. Then, unexpectedly, I felt the strangest sensation in my mind and body of what Ralph must be feeling—the pain of knowing how hurt his family was that loved him. He would be devastated knowing how the tragedy, the loss of him from our lives, affected us. He is so proud now, of all of us. The pain of my children's loss showed up next. I felt the hurt and pain they must be experiencing, and I so badly wanted to protect them from it. After a while, I became aware of extended family and friends and the grief they were experiencing. At first it was all about me and my pain, and then slowly and gently, more was revealed.

The first secondary loss I encountered was losing the ability to sleep in our bed, the bed we shared for thirty-seven years! I couldn't do it. I tried the first night, tossing and turning. I decided I would sleep on the couch in the family room. I slept there for at least three years, I on the big couch, and my dog, Charlie Jo, on the love seat. I left the TV on, barely paying attention to it, just to have the painful silence broken. I would fall asleep between eleven and midnight and wake up to some strange show or infomercial at two or three and turn off the TV. I was blessed to have slept well. I know some widow(er)s have the opposite problem -- of not being able to sleep. Thoughts I had during the day of break-ins or strange people outside, thankfully disappeared at night. It baffled me as I normally, in the past, was a big scaredy-cat. Ralph's presence was comforting me, allowing me to sleep restfully. I did sleep with the phone by my side, just in case.

Lots of people gave me ideas of how to get back in my bed. I rearranged furniture and had fun getting new bedding. It helped a little. But inviting someone to share your bed with you brings up challenges, even two to three years into the grief journey. Guilt, shame, and anger raise their ugly heads. I felt like Ralph spoke to me at one point: *It's OK to move on with your life, but not in our bed.* So down in the family room on an air mattress, lay my new friend and I. Eventually the bed became a safe and loving place to be.

The next secondary loss was comfort in familiar stomping grounds. Seeing all the places you frequented with your love triggers all kinds of emotions. I remember seeing restaurants, parks, beaches, bike paths, cider mills, and all the places we enjoyed together and I have memories of. They sparked a gut-level feeling of pain and yearning to have my Ralph back and experience it all again. Eating in the same restaurants can break your heart. I remember going in a local Mexican restaurant we enjoyed regularly. The waiter asked "How are you?" as I sat with two of my best friends. "Not well, my husband was killed while riding his bicycle, hit by a distracted driver." I pulled out a picture of him and showed the waiter. He remembered him and felt so bad. It warmed my heart that he remembered us. The first few months to a year or more, I would answer totally honestly. We must not be afraid to share our truth. We need to talk about our hurt and our pain, and educate others on what to say and do. We must not wear that fake smile, that fake mask, to not burden others with our pain. We need to create a society where expressing one's pain is not only accepted, but honored and encouraged. We are human beings—we feel, we hurt, we cry, and we scream in utter agony at the loss of a treasured loved one. Some of the places hurt really badly at first, but as time goes on and some healing has occurred, those places can become sweet memories.

Next, handling household issues, such as the refrigerator or washer not working, car maintenance, and yardwork, became a pain in the ass. I had so many things break down that first year. I was calling someone weekly. Things that my husband would just take care of, without me even knowing, became a big deal for me. It was hard, very difficult, for as I would call to have another man come into my house and fix what Ralph used to fix, surges of grief would fill my gut, heart, and soul. Anger and tears would pop up, asking, *Why are you gone? Where are you? Why did you leave me with this?*

Garbage pickup issues happened within the first couple of weeks. I had set out tons of garbage in the normal area in front of the house. After a while, I noticed it building up, so I phoned the garbage company and they said, "You did not pay your bill." *Sorry assholes, I was a little busy with a husband being killed and a funeral.* Really, I explained the situation and they did not care! This felt absurd, appalling, and showed a total lack of empathy. I scanned through the yellow pages and found a local garbage company. I phoned them, and as we spoke we both realized that I was speaking to the lady who had prayed over my husband's body as he lay on the pavement, right after being hit. Her husband would be right over and pick up the garbage, free of charge.

Insurance companies, utilities, and bills add other secondary burdens as one is trying to just breathe each minute of each day and cope with the loss. They become overwhelming. Kindnesses mixed with apathetic people who don't care, don't understand, and don't want to, create even more mixed emotions. Calling the electric company, the gas company, or the phone company to report the death makes matters worse most of the time, as the people who answer the phone are not trained. Several times I would say my husband was killed riding his bicycle, and no response, nothing. Do you believe this, in our society, our culture, that people, including who you thought were close friends and family, have no response to such a horrific event?! Sometimes I would get an empathetic response, other times a cold aloof, "I'm sorry to hear that." Credit-card companies create one hell of a mess, also. A lawyer I had through this tragedy handled the credit-card companies. Some amounts got lowered and some erased, but the worst were some saying I owed money when it was totally in my husband's name and they couldn't prove I was on it! This is still hurting my credit five years later! It is appalling what widows go through in the aftermath—just appalling!

Traveling alone after having a partner by your side for many years is quite an enlightening experience. I remember getting ready to head up to the cabin in northern Michigan, just Charlie Jo and I. Packing up the car hurt, literally hurt so badly emotionally that I almost froze. The excitement of being in my cabin, close to Lake Huron, moved me. I got the dog in the car and off we went. I always took the car to the dealership before any trip, just to make sure all was well. I had stayed at my cabin alone before, and I had flown on a plane and rented a car alone previously too, but it feels so different when that man, your husband, isn't available to answer the phone to help you if need be. You feel like no one has your back, and it's scary. Flying without him either by my side or at home felt really awkward. I remember walking through the airline terminals and feeling so lost, so alone, dragging my suitcase in the bathroom with me, holding back tears. After a few times, I got more and more used to it and more comfortable flying alone. You don't realize how much you count on someone for everyday living until they are gone.

Judith Finneren

Chapter Twelve
Travel Adventures

$\mathscr{A}$ s time went on and I got more used to it, traveling became a huge part of my healing process. My first travel adventure was October of 2011. Long before Ralph passed in July, I had planned on going to a women's conference at Enchantment Resort in Sedona, Arizona. Spirit told me that I must go, even though I felt numb, raw, and vulnerable from the sudden, tragic, loss of my love three months earlier.

To this day, I do not know how I got to the airport, got on the airplane, rented a car, and drove to Sedona from Phoenix. It must have been God and Spirit. I arrived at Enchantment, a secluded breathtaking resort nestled in the red rocks of West Sedona, around lunch time on a Saturday. Asking for help after parking the car, I found a group of women and joined them for lunch. I felt nervous and scared to share my truth of the last few months with strangers. Still, I spoke up right away about what my life had been like during that time. I received what I needed: love, caring, and support. I felt heard and validated.

Later that day, Clarissa Pinkola Estes, speaker and author of *Women Who Run with Wolves*, had us write questions on index cards. We threw them in a basket for her to choose from and answer in front of the audience of about 200 women. I wrote my truth, as I had no energy to do otherwise. I wrote, "What does one do when a husband of thirty-seven years was suddenly tragically killed ten weeks ago?" I thought, if she reads this, she will not answer it. She will throw it back in the basket and ignore it. She picked it up and read it aloud, much to my surprise and glee, for I really did need an answer. She asked that the person who wrote this to please come up to the stage. I felt humbled and honored that she read my card and then asked me to come forward. I walked up there, and with her complete and utter caring and compassion, I felt listened to, cared about, and loved. I felt for that moment that only we two existed, even though lots of women were present. It was an amazing experience and part of my healing journey. After a few minutes, when we finished talking, she asked someone who was seated near my empty seat to come forward and walk me back. I later found out that her name was Janet.

When Clarissa was done speaking that day, so many of these women came up to me and shared their stories of grief with me. I was so touched and honored, and they gave me hope. Janet, the person who walked me back to my seat, became, and remains to this day, one of my best friends and also a big part of my healing journey. We later went to Mexico together and explored islands and cities I had never heard of. What a fun and glorious time it was. Healing was taking place even more, creating new memories to replace painful ones.

Traveling to Pensacola, Florida, with my brother and sister-in-law came next in February 2012, seven months post-trauma, and was also a very healing experience. I remember walking on the beach with Sue, my sister-in-law, and she asked me a question I sure did not expect. It went something like this: "Are you able to name three good things that have happened, three things you have learned since Ralph's death?" *Wow*. I was flabbergasted.

"What? Nothing good has happened," I said. When the initial surge of anger subsided, I thought about it and did come up with three things. I am able to do things on my own -- and quite well -- was one. I have a financial advisor I trust, who just seemed to show up in my life at the right time. God also provided dog sitters I trust completely to watch over my precious dog, Charlie Jo, so that I am able to travel and not worry.

I spent precious time with my brother, having breakfast at a cute little restaurant across from the condo we were staying at. Many walks and talks on the beach were helpful to me and having family nearby was truly a gift. I remember carrying the weight of the grief, and it felt dark and heavy. As I walked and talked it became lighter. At times the darkness and heaviness would creep back, and as time went on, lightness seemed to take over.

In the spring of 2013, Janet and I gifted ourselves with seeing the Dalai Lama in New Orleans. We had to wait in a super long line for about an hour. When we finally were able to get in and sit down with thousands of others, we heard chanting and Tibetan music. The Dalai Lama came out and spoke. His spirit was palpable, his essence touched me, even though I found it very difficult to understand most of his words.

Of course, while in New Orleans, we had to go to Café Du Monde and enjoy a cup of coffee while tantalizing our tongues with the taste of a square piece of dough, fried and covered with powdered sugar; better known as a beignet.

We then traveled to Northern California for a week-long event called Spirit Quest. We slept in a tent and one night the temperature dropped so low that I was freezing. I mentioned it to others the next day and received so many blankets for the rest of the time that I didn't have to worry one bit about being cold again. We experienced many talks around the campfire. At one point, I was assigned to be the "fire keeper" from 9 p.m. to midnight. That meant I had to put logs on the fire and not let it go out. That was a fun experience. We shared meals together, all of us helping with cooking or cleaning up. We attended ceremonies at the campfire, too. Sage and sweet grass were used for smudging as we entered the circle around the fire. The lady in charge would call in the spirits of the ancestors to be with us and lead us in healing activities. Two or three hours later, she would thank the spirits for being present and send them off. I felt in an altered state while I was there. It was an interesting and educational experience.

The summer of 2013, after completing film school and arriving back in Michigan, was a time I decided I would mostly spend at my cabin in the woods in East Tawas. I love East Tawas and have lots of fun family-and-friend memories there. The cabin was mine now. My parents had bought it when I was twelve years old. Then Ralph and I bought it from my dad some years later after my mother had passed. Now, with Ralph gone, Charlie Jo and I would enjoy the summer there.

One surprise I had was seeing my cousin as she was driving by. We chatted and I found out she lived right down the street from me on Lake Huron. What an unexpected surprise and joy. She invited me to the delightful Tawas Bay Yacht Club, where she was a member. I went and met some friendly folks. She suggested I walk up and down the dock and see if anyone needed crew members for sailing. I found the most fun pair of guys. I began sailing with them almost every Saturday or Sunday. We were in a race and came in second. Oh, my gosh, was it fun! Friends came up to visit, and we had bonfires, chasing mosquitoes away. Northern Michigan is pure delight!

Another joy I experienced that summer was spending time with my aunt and uncle, my cousin's parents. They lived in a cabin on an inland lake about 30 miles away. My cousin and I enjoyed dinner with them a couple of times. They are in their eighties now, and with huge hugs and tears we greeted one another. It was a healing experience I needed and treasure.

Fall of 2013 brought a wedding invitation, my nephew's destination wedding in Playa del Carmen. I was excited, because my friend Janet was living in Merida, Mexico, at the time, and she was coming to meet me. It was interesting flying into the little airport in Mexico, in Cancun, I believe it was. There were so many people standing around with signs and speaking Spanish. I did not understand a word. I walked to the baggage claim and awaited my luggage, which also was very different, as lots of people around were only speaking Spanish. I felt very alone in a foreign country. Where were all the Americans? I arrived about an hour or so before Janet, so I managed to find a restaurant nearby, have a refreshing cold drink and some lunch, and await her arrival. I was so happy to be meeting up with my dear friend, my children who were flying in from Washington, D.C., with their partners, and of course my nephew who was getting married, his beautiful future bride, my brother, and his family. The resort was exquisite! A gorgeous swimming pool wound around the resort as well, and the beach was just unbelievable. I never saw what looked like beds on a beach before. They were amazing. Lying there tanning or in the shade to catch a wink of sleep with sounds of the sea in your ears was a gift. The wedding took place on the beach with the sight and sound of ocean waves as background. We spent time together laughing, talking, celebrating, and enjoying life.

Janet and I then went to Merida, where she was living temporarily. It was a four-hour bus ride from Playa del Carmen. We arrived at an old Mexican town with narrow streets and vendors selling all kinds of tantalizing food. We walked about a block to get fresh bottled water, for use at her little apartment. We visited smaller coastal towns, such as Progreso, enjoyed the beach and a bite to eat. I loved it there! We also took a boat to Cozumel and Isla Mujeres. Isla Mujeres means "Island of Women." What a special time, renting an old Volkswagen in Cozumel to get us around to explore the Island and renting a pink golf cart that allowed us to visit the various sightseeing areas of Isla Mujeres with its strong surf and rocky coast. This all took place two years and three months after my traumatic loss. I tell you this: it is OK to live, have fun, and engage in life while also grieving. I used to say, "I am putting grief on the back burner for now."

I cannot leave Mexico until I share with you one of the most awesome experiences I have ever had, that of swimming in a "cenote," an underwater sinkhole. It is estimated that there are more than 6,000 in the Yucatan. They were once the only source for sweet, fresh water in the local jungle. For the Mayas, they were considered sacred places. The sun filtering in through holes above the cave-like areas give the cenote a magical feel. The crystal-clear turquoise color of the water, with a very comfortable temperature of 78 degrees, creates an incredibly pleasant experience. I want to go back there right now. If you ever get a chance, check them out. It is truly worth it.

Another experience Janet and I shared was back near Sedona, Arizona. We went on what was referred to as a Catayak tour (so called because the boat is a kayak crossed with a catamaran). We cruised down the Colorado River, about a dozen of us in all. We saw mule deer all over the sides of the mountains. I'm baffled by how they balance themselves. Arriving at our camping area, we unloaded our gear, picked a spot, set up camp and explored the area. Down the path a ways was an incredible water area. It was like a small river, divided into sections, beginning with a very cold little pond, leading up to a sixth larger pond of hot water. Each pond in between the first and sixth was progressively warmer than the last. It was amazing and totally natural. The following day we boarded the Catayak and headed toward the Hoover Dam. Stopping a distance before, we hopped off the boat and ascended to a natural sauna. It was really cool! I felt too hot and too closed in, so I exited pretty quickly. For those who enjoy saunas, it's quite lovely.

In June of 2014 I decided to go to Alaska, a place I have wanted to visit for years. I would get this brochure a couple times a year from a shaman I had done a sweat lodge with several years ago in my home state of Michigan. I would read it over and think, *Man, I would love to do one of these trips.* Well in early 2014, I got the brochure and began planning my trip to Alaska. It was awesome. Bears, whales, sea otters, and the Mendenhall glacier were some of the highlights. I stayed in a log cabin in the woods with two ladies who ended up becoming great friends. There was no bathroom, and, in the middle of the night, we had to walk across a dirt road, flashlight in hand, to use the outhouse. "Haha, the heck with that," I said after the first night, and stooped outside the cabin to relieve myself, fearing the whole time that a bear may want to befriend me.

The shaman did a spirit ceremony with me and the group, involving my Ralph, wherein we all sat in a circle. I sat next to the shaman with an altar before us. The altar was made up of a sacred blanket with sacred objects on it, such as feathers, rocks, sage and sweet grass that the shaman used during the ceremony. I felt a letting go, and a sense of Ralph's spirit soaring with the eagles as the shaman spoke of setting Ralph's spirit free. It was reverent and, again, a time I will never forget as part of my healing journey. Letting go and moving forward began to have real meaning, as I was experiencing just that.

I traveled to Washington, D.C., several times alone to visit with my children. I found myself afraid, even though I had traveled alone before. I had not traveled to D.C. alone—Ralph was always with me. So this was a first. I found doing things for the first time alone, that I had always done with my partner prior to his death, was a challenge and a positive growth experience. It was a challenge due to the fear I felt and thoughts of, *how am I going to do this alone?*

I remember one time when I was taking a train and then a bus to the airport. I was flying out of Baltimore, so it involved more than just a metro ride from a subway station in the city to the airport. My daughter was figuring out what train for me to get on, and it was a little frantic getting to the answer. Once we figured it out, she walked me right onto the train and said goodbye, and I just sobbed. I could feel my nerves, my fear, and all kinds of mixed emotions. My feelings of insecurity were high, and I felt so damned alone. Leaving my children to go home to an empty house was extremely difficult. I knew this was just a phase I was going through with the grief so fresh, and I reassured my daughter that I just needed her to be by my side and help me a little more right now. The positive growth came from the feeling of joy and excitement that I met the challenge, that I did it, and survived. My confidence and sense of security rose. Eventually I was flying into Reagan International Airport by myself, hopping on the metro to a station near their home, walking a few blocks, suitcase and backpack in hand, and arriving on their doorstep. I am telling you, that felt extremely good! They were proud of their mama too!

Judith Finneren

Chapter Thirteen
Not A Monster

At first I wanted to kill him. He had destroyed our lives. He had sucked every goddamn ounce of life and hope from my body! I didn't know if I would ever be the same again. I questioned my sanity often. I knew that was normal when one experiences deep grief, so I knew I was OK. The disbelief, the shock, and the fear, were so prevalent and still sometimes visit me. I needed as much help as I could get. I vented to friends, family, and therapists and wrote about it in my daily journaling. It helped.

The first day I saw him was in the courthouse. I was a wreck and needed to see who this monster was. Every twenty-six-year-old-looking man I saw, I thought was him. I was sitting in a little conference room right off the hallway on the second floor, talking to the prosecutor and the sheriff. They knew I was anxious to see who the person was who destroyed our family's life.

The sheriff saw him and pointed him out through the half-closed door. I cringed at the sight of him. I felt so many emotions at once. Hate, anger, sadness, and a sense of relief washed over me, as I finally was seeing the man who killed my Ralph. He was late arriving. That did not sit well with me. His mother and father were with him. He looked a little frightened and nervous. We entered the courtroom of the female judge. Other cases were being called, too. Finally, his name was called. As I walked out of the building, I saw his parents inside out of the corner of my eye, so Spirit told me, *Walk back in*. I was so nervous I was shaking. I walked up to them and remember hearing the mother say, "We were going to send you a card, and we didn't know what to do." They apologized. I said, "It's not too late." I have never to this day received anything from them. I felt hurt and angry. It makes me wonder, do they not care or are they paralyzed with a sense of inadequacy? Are they thinking the harm they caused was so enormous that nothing they could think of was good enough, so they ended up doing nothing at all? I ended up feeling unsupported in my time of need.

Another time—I believe it was the sentencing date—my children flew in from Washington, D.C. They held a picture of their dad while I spoke of our gut-wrenching, heart-breaking, unbelievable loss. "Victim's statement," I believe it was called. It felt good to let him know what he stole from us. The judge said, "There is no amount of money that can replace a life." She was empathetic and concerned. It seems like we went to the courthouse several times.

Eventually, he got sentenced. At my request, the sentence consisted of some jail time, working on the side of the road picking up garbage so he would feel the cars racing by his body, and, most of all, I requested he attend a Ride of Silence. The first year, 2012, he did not attend a Ride of Silence. I wanted him to attend the one I was going to, to satisfy my desire to see him there, honoring those bicyclists killed or injured while bicycling. I neglected to be that specific, so the next year he was ordered to attend, and he said he went to one nearby his house. I to this day do not know if he actually ever went. His probation officer said he did. I spoke with his probation officer periodically. He had to pay some minuscule amount of money to the court, and the charge was a misdemeanor, a "moving violation causing death."

At some point, the judge asked me, in the courtroom, if I had anything else to say or questions to ask. I said, "Yes," and looked at him. "What were you doing when you hit my Ralph?" The judge asked if we wanted to go into a conference room, just the two of us, so off we went. What happened next is one of the most heart-wrenching, down-to-earth, spiritual events I have ever experienced. We sat across from one another. I was feeling tense and nervous, and again, I asked, "What were you doing?" He said, "I was looking in my backseat, making sure I had everything for work, my lunchbox and things." I responded, "We don't know why these things happen." I cannot recall the rest of the conversation, but we ended with an embrace and tears. I felt compassion. He was no longer a monster, but a young man distracted while driving.

At some point, I had to attend what they call a "restitution hearing." When I first heard of it, I had no idea what that meant. It involved him paying me money. I remember having to sit in the witness box and answer questions by the prosecutor and public defense attorneys. At one point, the defense attorney questioned my need for counseling the rest of my life. I said, "I am a licensed professional counselor who just experienced the sudden tragic death of her spouse. I *will* need counseling the rest of my life."

He quieted down immediately. That I had to prove why restitution makes sense for me is unbelievable. I had no idea that was going to happen, that I was being called to "testify!" "Restitution" meant "recompense for injury or loss." As the judge stated previously, no amount of money would replace the loss of a human life. I will tell you what it does do for me. The amount of money I receive lets me know that he cares, that he realizes to some extent what he did to my life and my children's lives. When he was first ordered to pay, he didn't.

We had to go to court several times before he finally understood. At this point, the judge, who had previously sentenced him, was tired of seeing him and his lack of accepting responsibility. She asked for him and me to go to the conference room and figure things out or she would. Wow, that caught me off guard.

So off we went to talk. I spoke from my heart and explained to him that every time he did not pay, it felt like a knife to my heart. It made me feel like he didn't care. He looked at me and said, "I didn't know that. I am sorry. I am different now." He has paid me weekly now for a couple of years with no problems. For me to get to the point of talking to him as a human being—not as a monster and not as a killer—took a lot of personal in-depth psychological and spiritual work. It definitely was an inside job. I had to work through the anger.

I journaled and spoke with several people, expressing my feelings over and over. These feelings and thoughts changed every time I told my story. I was healing. I had to realize that this young man did not get up that day with the intention of killing my husband, changing the lives of so many, including his own. I was searching for an answer, a reason, an explanation that would make sense of all this. I still think about it at times, not ever knowing why my husband was killed, yet accepting the mystery of it all. We are all dealt hands in this life, and we make the most of the cards we are dealt. As my feelings changed toward him, forgiveness showed up.

The last time we saw each other was at a local Starbucks two years ago. I was nervous about seeing him, not sure how I would react, wondering if he would even show up. I arrived first, and moments later he walked in. I felt a sense of relief when I saw him. I was thinking to myself, he cares, we are going to handle this. He showed me the paper he was submitting to his payroll department at work, to have his restitution automatically deducted. He explained how the process works. He is in charge of this, not the courts, so if at any time he falters on payments we may have to go back to court. He is a little older and wiser now, so I hope and pray that he continues to understand the impact of his distracted driving, that of destroying a family. He has two children and they all remain in my prayers, for the children need a healthy father.

Judith Finneren

Chapter Fourteen
Support Grieving Loved Ones

*I*nvite us to outings of any sort: dinner, baseball games, walks in the park, swimming—just be with us, sit with us quietly, and let us be, in our grief, with you present and witnessing it. If you are comfortable, ask to hold and hug us, ask us what we are thinking about, speak the name of the beloved who died, and ask about special memories. Don't try to make us feel better by not validating the reality of now, which is the experience of deep sorrowful grief. Some common errors people unwittingly make are saying things like, "You're young—you will fall in love again," "He got out of your way," or "He is in a better place." "He is in a better place" drives me nuts, and I think, *No, he is not in a better place—his place is here with me and our children.*

Rather than suggest that the grieving person call you, call them, check in on them, drop by. I know I was not able to think straight and make decisions; I barely wanted to move my body, let alone think to call someone. I had several Post-it notes on the wall with names and numbers, but I experienced what I call "grief paralysis": sitting, feeling numb, unable to move, and feeling no motivation or inspiration at all. Getting out helped me open doors just a little bit to life again even when I really did not feel like it.

I say "remember his name" for many reasons. One is I want others to know how special it is for us, the mourners, the ones who have lost a beloved, to hear the name of that person spoken. Even seeing it written in emails or messages is such a wonderful blessing. Some people say, "Oh, I didn't want to say anything that might bring up your pain or make you cry." Let me tell you, we are thinking of him always and forever. Not a day goes by that I don't think of Ralph, my husband of thirty-seven years and father of our two beautiful children. When you say his name and let me know that you remember him, the warmth in my soul is heightened. One of our biggest fears as grieving people is that everyone will forget our beloved.

I really do not like hearing about other people's wedding anniversaries. Of course, I am happy for them, but it hurts badly and only reminds me of what I don't have. But let me know you remember him on our anniversary and on Father's Day and birthdays. His Angelversary (the day he died) is an especially important day to acknowledge the deceased person's name, that they were once here on this planet, with us, among us, and that their life here mattered. We miss him! Nov. 16, 1974, Ralph and I were married. Death did not end that uniting of hearts and souls. I will be thinking of him on that date more than ever. Don't hesitate to say "happy anniversary" to me, even if I have a second love in my life now. It's OK. It is all about love, always.

Judith Finneren

Chapter Fifteen
Words For
Those Grieving

*I*f you have recently lost a loved one, please have hope, don't ever give up, keep your mind and heart open, try new things, step out of your comfort zone, and discover who you are, maybe for the first time ever. Marvel at the miracle that is you. Share in such wondrous joy of the life you have created. I found that as old friends seemed to slowly disappear from my life, new ones showed up, new ones that matched my new vibrational level, my new zest for life. I found a deeper, more profound intimate connection with others, and I loved it! So carry on, my friend, and know you will continue to heal. As grief changes shape, so shall you and your precious gift of life. Prosper and grow old, my friend, for the day has come to reach, to satisfy yearnings withheld for so many years.

Play pool, poker, ping pong—just play, have fun, enjoy and be "in joy;" be wonderful and full of wonder. Getting out helps open doors just a little bit to life again. When you are in grief paralysis, at the very least, go to your mailbox. Walk to your mailbox or the end of your driveway if your mailbox is right by your door. Those of us in semi-rural to rural areas have to walk to the end of our driveway to check our mailbox. Some days, that is all I was able to do.

Alone times will occur; there will be days with no one else around, and, oh, that deafening silence in the house, that used to be so full of love and life, just made me sob and cry out loud to God, "Why have you forsaken me? Please, please help me!" Sometimes while driving, Spirit had me say, "I am love; I am light; I am all one. We are love; we are light; we are all one." I would raise my right hand up to the heavens while saying the above words.

Do it for you, live your life, and be open to receive the gifts that await you. You are worthy of the best, so please don't settle—no settling—speak up, and be yourself now and forever. "Let it Be" by the Beatles kept me motivated and inspired during this grief/growth journey as I felt the presence of Mother Mary. Listen to that song, my friends, and take it into your heart and soul. Shed tears, let the sacred pain and sorrow release from deep within. "Bridge Over Troubled Water" by Simon and Garfunkel helped ease my pain also, as I thought of God as my bridge. Use songs, play music, sit in sacred silence, and do what you need to do for you, to comfort you. I am practicing playing a Native American flute now, and so enjoying it. It brings me peace, comfort, and a sense of sacredness that I so need. You have it in you, I know you do! Remember His name, too. This touches a deep spot within me, the name of God, a higher power, Mother Nature, something bigger than ourselves. Spirit guides, blessed Mother-Father God and guardian angels, along with archangels Michael, Gabriel, and Raphael have helped me travel this journey of grief, loss, hope, and healing. I *know* that outside forces have helped me to participate in activities and relationships that would aid in further growth and healing. I felt led to make a film, to write this book, and to do a triathlon. I am being led. As long as I keep my heart and mind open, I will hear the voices of hope, see and experience the miracles, and continually meet and see angels on my path. So I say to you, please remember his name and please remember His name.

If you are blessed to be creating a new relationship, do not compare what this person is doing with what your spouse used to do. After over thirty years with the same person, we get used to how special days were celebrated. It helps to talk about and, in a compassionate way, discuss how each of you would like to celebrate, even share old memories. Widow-widower relationships share a very unique past. Sharing precious lives with one another creates an interesting and challenging situation at times. We did not break up, divorce, or leave each other intentionally. We still loved our spouses very, very much. It takes some new special skills to be in that place with each other, to hear about the past with compassion and empathy, not jealousy and anger. I sometimes will suggest talking about it later, depending on what mood I am in at the time. Validating each other's experience is a true gift. One of the fun, neat things that happens when you get involved in a new relationship is you begin to feel like a teenager again. Going out, dating and experiencing new things together is such a joy. Keep moving forward. You are not alone.

I hope and I pray that this book of my experiences and tips on getting through the loss of a loved one along with strength and hope have helped you. Happy trails to you, my friends.

And as Ralph said in one of the last messages to our daughter,

"THE FUTURE IS BRIGHT!"

Judith Finneren

Epilogue

$\mathcal{T}$hese are some cherished moments since I lost my beloved Ralph that I want to share with you. My son and I went to Lake Placid in 2014 to watch my daughter participate in an Ironman event. It was awesome. We shared so many fun moments. The first evening, as we were walking down the street, my children had me close my eyes, and then look. There in front of me was Dancing Bears restaurant. Oh, my gosh, "Dancing Bear" was Ralph's nickname. I was touched and warmed as I felt a smile come across my face. We played on the river and enjoyed endless root beer floats at the local A&W and, to my surprise, I got to medal my daughter. What does "medal my daughter" mean? It means I got to go into the finish line area, a VIP area, and for her completion of this wondrous feat of swimming, bicycling, and running, place the finisher medal around her neck, and give her a big hug from her dad and me. I felt Ralph's presence as compassion, love, and joy. His spirit gave me tingles as I placed that medal around her neck. The date was July 27th, the anniversary of her dad's death. I am writing this as the fifth Father's Day without him has just passed. I forgot for a moment how much it hurts. Memories flash back and roll down my cheeks. My children are not with me to honor him, so we acknowledge our loss on Facebook, by sharing photos and sweet memories. Holli put a picture up of her and her dad from her college days at Georgia Southern. I cried from such a deep place of grief and loss when I saw it. I put up two photos, one of the ghost bike and one of myself wearing the finisher medal I had received the day before at my first triathlon.

I finished not only for myself, but for him too, as he was killed while training for one. The deep loss began pouring out of me in sobs as I embarked on the last two miles of the event. I was walking and the emotion just washed over me like waves in the sea. I composed myself after a time and talked with my friend as he walked with me. When I got closer to that finish line, hearing the crowd and the sound of the announcer saying, "Here comes our next athlete," energy arose in my body like I have never felt before. I began running, then running faster as the cheers went right to my heart. The wave of emotions broke through again, like a tsunami in tears of love, hope, and tremendous joy. I had completed a dream for both of us. Ralph was right there with me the whole time. I felt it and I knew it.

Note To Ralph

I am so very grateful the universe allowed us to share some time together and create two of the most compassionate human beings I have ever known. Sail on, my dear sweet Ralphy. Ride that bicycle through the heavens. People down here on Earth keep being hit and killed on their bikes. Please get something going in heaven and reach us here on Earth to help. I will be doing my third triathlon soon. Your son is enjoying sailing. I see you in him. He is teaching the sport to others in Taiwan, racing sailboats with friends and is buying a thirty-nine-footer to embark on a journey around the world with his beautiful, adventurous wife. She loves China too, just like you did. What great conversations you would have had. Your daughter has participated in many Ironmans and is going to Kona this year! We are going to Kona, Ralphy! Do you believe it! Dreams are coming true. I see you in her, too. I know you are so proud of all of us. Life is good, Ralphy. Thank you! We miss you! Carry on, my angel warrior. We love you and always will; carrying you in our hearts forever.

About The Author

$\mathcal{J}$udith Finneren, licensed professional counselor, holds a bachelor of science degree in elementary education and a master of arts degree in counseling from Oakland University in Rochester, Michigan. For twenty-four years, she has helped people overcome addictions, depression, anxiety, grief, and other obstacles that block the road to peace, contentment, and happiness. As a certified Imago relationship therapist, she has helped numerous couples find their joy again. Trained in bioenergetics therapy as well, Judith loves to free up blockages in clients' energy through talk and movement, enhancing their passion for life and ability to live from the heart.

Judith holds a digital filmmaking certificate from Yavapai College in Sedona, Arizona, where, after the death of her husband, she created an award-winning documentary titled *Ghostbike*, which has been showing at several film festivals throughout the United States.

For her and her beautiful adult children, a son and a daughter, conquering grief and accepting joy has been an ongoing process since the tragic death of a dear husband and wonderful father. Learning from each other, while loving and supporting one another, they each have moved forward enjoying life to the fullest.

Judith was born in Detroit, Michigan and currently resides in Lake Orion, Michigan where she enjoys hiking, bicycling, and kayaking with a new love, Gary, and her charming sweet dog Charlie Jo. Judith loves traveling and has recently spent time in Beijing, China; Dublin, Ireland; and Bruges, Belgium.

Resources

Kristine Carlson
www.kristinecarlson.com

Sarah McLean
www.mcleanmeditation.com

Christina Rasmussen
www.secondfirsts.com

Enocha Ranjita Ryan
www.yourheartshome.com

For more information about my book and film,
please visit my web site, www.judithfinneren.com